Survival Guides You Didn't Know You Needed

SURVIVING ON A DESERT ISLAND

Thomas Kingsley Troupe

BLACK RABBIT BOOKS

Hi Jinx is published by Black Rabbit Books
P.O. Box 3263, Mankato, Minnesota, 56002.
www.blackrabbitbooks.com
Copyright © 2018 Black Rabbit Books

Marysa Storm, editor; Michael Sellner, designer;
Catherine Cates, production designer;
Omay Ayres, photo researcher

Cataloging-in-Publication Data is available at the
Library of Congress.
ISBN 978-1-68072-342-7 (library binding)
ISBN 978-1-68072-372-4 (e-book)

Printed in China. 9/17

Image Credits

Dreamstime: Regissercom, 8 (right crab); iStock: drmakkoy, Cover (island,
bkgd); ValeriyaRedina, 12 (sand); Shutterstock: Alhovik, 21 (gecko); anfisa
focusova, 3 (bkgd), 12 (bkgd); Angeliki Vel, 8 (sun); Arcady, 3 (note), 6
(note); articular, 2–3 (tree); Artisticco, 4 (exhaust); Art Painter, 18–19 (sand);
Big Boy, 11 (top left bird); Daniel Wiedemann, 1, 23 (fish); Danilo Sanino,
11 (top r bird); dedMazay, 4 (shark); Dreamcreation, Cover (piranha);
Dualororua, 11 (tree), 16; ekler, 13; frescomovie, Back Cover (bkgd); 11
(bkgd); GraphicsRF, 4 (island, plane, water), 14–15 (whale, bkgd), 18–19
(branches); Ilya Chalyuk, 5, 9, 13 (marker strokes), 17, 20 (marker strokes);
John Langton, 8 (left crab), 20 (crab); John T Takai, 6 (fin); Memo Angeles,
4 (shark), 11 (boy, leaves), 12 (boy), 15 (fish); MintoGrina, 21 (footprints);
Mjosedesign, 7 (island); Moriz, Cover (child), 7 (child); Muhammad Desta
Laksana, 18 (turtle), 19 (lizard); Nyamol Ds, 11 (bottom bird); opicobello, 8
(marker), 10; Pasko Maksim, Back Cover (top); 9 (bottom), 23 (top); Pitju,
21 (curled corner); Regissercom, 8 (center crab); Ron Leishman, Cover
(bird), 7 (bird); SlipFloat, Cover (shark); Tanyastock, 18–19 (plane);
Teguh Mujiono, 19 (crab); Tony Oshlick, 8 (castle); Vaniatka, 14 (fish);
VectorShots, 14 (octopus, shrimp); Verzzh, 14–15 (kid); https://
commons. wikimedia.org: John Knight/U.S. Navy, 20 (photo) Every
effort has been made to contact copyright holders for material
reproduced in this book. Any omissions will be rectified in
subsequent printings if notice is given to the publisher.

CONTENTS

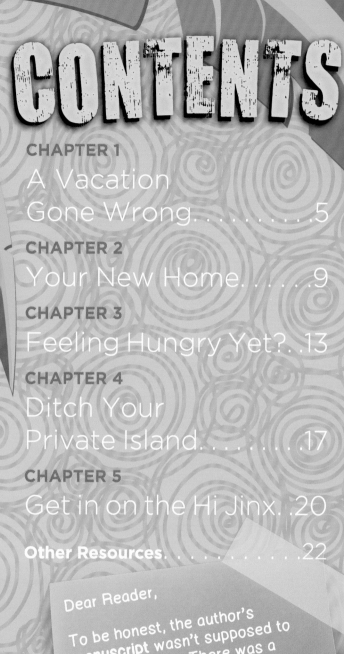

Dear Reader,

To be honest, the author's **manuscript** wasn't supposed to become a book. There was a horrible mix up. You can keep reading, if you want. Just don't take any of these suggestions seriously.

Sincerely,
a very sorry editor

Chapter 1
A VACATION GONE WRONG

You're flying to your **tropical** vacation. You imagine the white, sandy beaches. Palm trees will sway in the breeze. Waves will splash against the sand. It'll truly be paradise on earth.

Too bad you didn't get there! Your plane had engine trouble. It crashed on a **desert** island. It could happen, you know. You could end up stuck on a desert island!*

Editor's Note: It's highly unlikely this will happen to you.

Time to Survive!

A desert island can be a scary place. There's nowhere to go. There's nothing to eat. And the odds of surviving are slim.

Thankfully, you're prepared. You've got a survival guide you never thought you'd need. It's time to survive being stranded on a desert island!

Islands for You to Get Stuck On

Clipperton Island
(in the Pacific Ocean)

Great Blasket Island
(in the Atlantic Ocean)

Henderson Island
(in the South Pacific Ocean)

Survival List

Essential Sandcastle Building Tools

coconut bucket
water
dreams
lots and lots of sand

8

Chapter 2
YOUR NEW HOME

There's no one else on the island.
That makes you king or queen.
As royalty, you'll need a castle. With a
little water and sand, you can build
the perfect home.

Your castle will protect you from
the sun. It'll be a place to hang out too.
And the best part? You can build
a sandcastle inside your sandcastle.

The world's largest sandcastle was
more than 40 feet (12 meters) tall.

Palm Tree Fort

Sadly, the ocean's changing **tides** might ruin everything. The waves could wash away your castle. For a stronger shelter, consider a tree fort. The island view will be fantastic.

Grab some branches. No hammer and nails? No problem!* Use vines to tie the shelter together. You'll soon have a nice place to live.

A coconut tree can produce more than 50 coconuts a year.

*Editor's Note: No hammer and nails is definitely a problem.

*Editor's Note: Do you think the author really tried a sand sandwich?

Chapter 3
FEELING
HUNGRY YET?

Planning a meal on a desert island is no picnic. Aside from coconuts, there isn't much to eat. No matter how hungry you are, don't eat a sand sandwich. It's not healthy and tastes terrible.* You'll get sand stuck in your teeth too.

November 3rd is National Sandwich Day in the United States.

Seafood

Since a sandwich isn't an option, how about some seafood? Build a fishing rod, and dinner is served! But then you need a cooking fire. How can you get one of those?

Skip the fishing idea. The ocean is happy to **provide** other options! Sample a seaweed salad. Try some coral on the cob. The options are endless!

Chapter 4
DITCH YOUR PRIVATE ISLAND

Eventually, you'll want to leave the island. This part may be tricky. But where there's a will, there's a way.

Do whales love beaches? Maybe. Sometimes they try to lie in the sand. Sadly, beached whales can't get themselves back in the water. Help them back into the water. They might give you a ride off the island!*

Survival List
Top Places to Spot Whales

Alaska (in the United States)
Isle of Mull (in Scotland)
The Maldives (in South Asia)
Western Cape (in South Africa)

*Editor's Note: What the author didn't mention is how heavy whales are. A blue whale weighs about 150 tons (136 metric tons).

Signal for Help

No whales? No problem. Make a sign on the beach with some branches. With luck and patience, people in a passing plane will see it. They'll send for help.

You can also start writing! Write a polite note asking for help. Stick it in a bottle. Toss it in the ocean. You remembered to bring a bottle, right? If so, you're home free!*

In 2014, a man pulled a bottle from the Baltic Sea. The bottle had a message inside. It was more than 100 years old.

Being stuck on a desert island isn't fun. It's lonely, and there's too much sand. This useful guide will help you survive your island adventure.

Editor's Note: This is a terrible idea. It might take years for someone to find the bottle.

Chapter 5

GET IN ON THE HI JINX

The chances of being stranded on a desert island are slim. But it does happen. In 2016, three men were tossed from their boat into the ocean. They ended up on Fanadik, a desert island. They were there for three days. Using palm **fronds**, they spelled out "HELP." People in a plane saw the sign. The Coast Guard rescued the men.

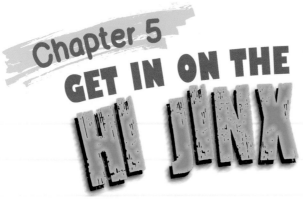

Take It One Step More

1. Imagine you are stranded on a desert island. What would you do to pass the time?

2. You won't see people on a desert island. But you might see some animals. Research animals that live on desert islands.

3. What do you think the author of this book was thinking? If his suggestions are crazy, why did he write the book?

GLOSSARY

desert (DEZ-ert)—a place with very few or no people

frond (FROND)—a large, long leaf

manuscript (MAN-yuh-skript)—the original copy of a book before it has been printed

provide (pruh-VAHYD)—to supply something that is wanted or needed

tide (TAHYD)—the rise and fall of waters in the ocean

tropical—(TROP-i-kuhl)—something related to the tropics

BOOKS

Boothroyd, Jennifer. *Let's Visit the Ocean.* Biome Explorers. Minneapolis: Lerner Publications, 2017.

Jenner, Caryn. *Shipwreck.* DK Adventures. New York: DK, Penguin Random House, 2015.

Perish, Patrick. *Survive on a Desert Island.* Survival Zone. Minneapolis: Bellwether Media, Inc., 2017.

WEBSITES

Coconut Facts for Kids
www.sciencekids.co.nz/sciencefacts/food/coconuts.html

Island Facts
www.softschools.com/facts/geography/island_facts/2229/

Islands
nationalgeographic.org/media/satellite-imagery-islands/

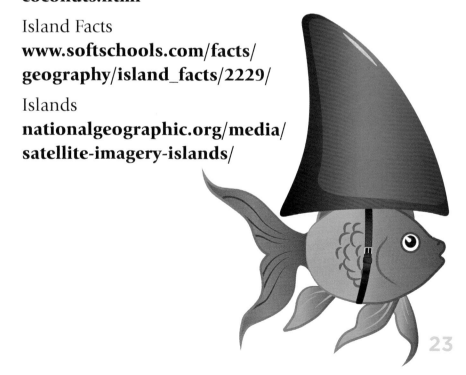

INDEX